Contents

Open Wide!

Written by Avelyn Davidson

Not me.
My teeth
are clean.

Not me.
My teeth are clean.

4

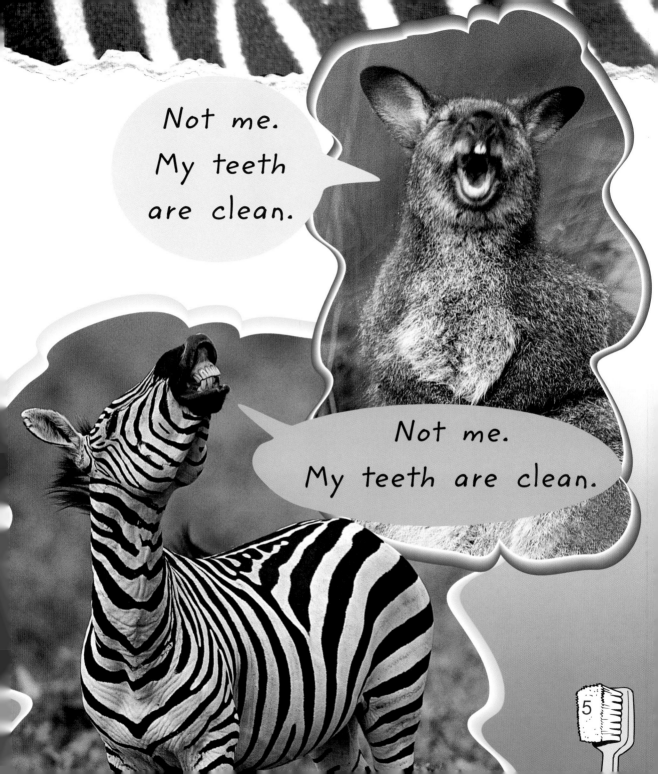

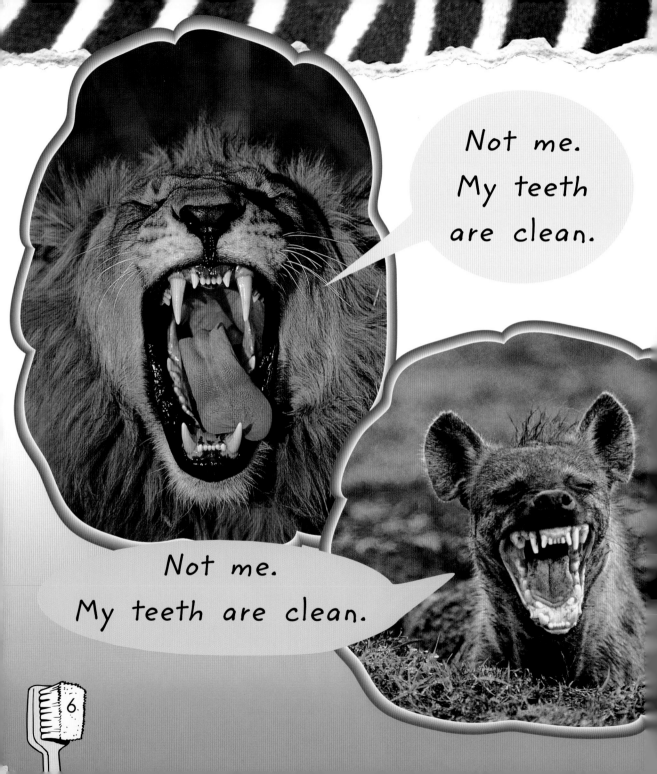

Make a Snake

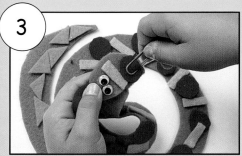

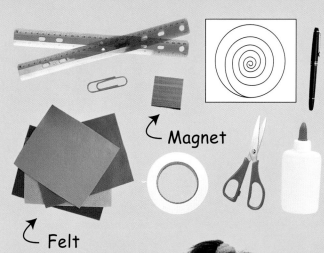

Magnet

Felt

Animal Antics!

What animals can you find in this picture?

Which animals are farm animals?

Which animals are zoo animals?

Which animal would you like for a pet?

What can you see that begins with the letter **d**?

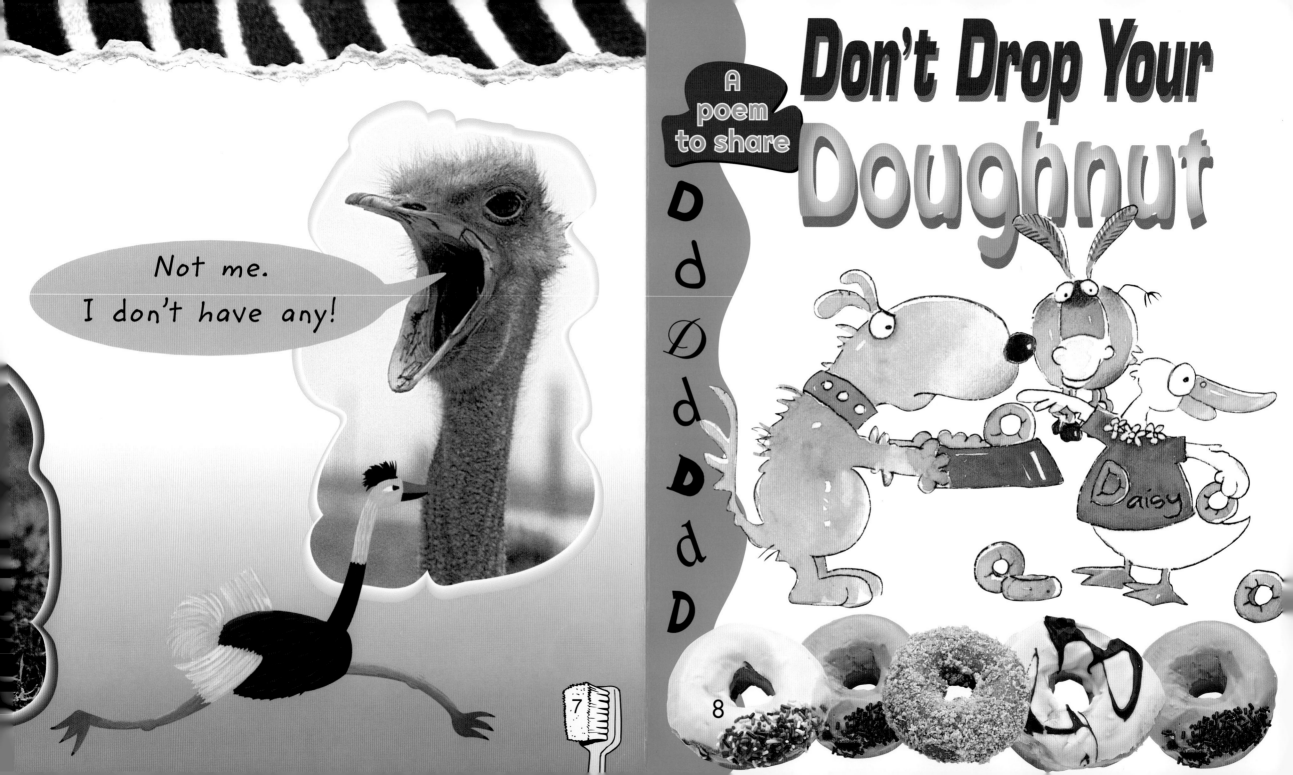

Not me.
I don't have any!

7

A poem to share

Don't Drop Your Doughnut

D D D D D D D

8

Daisy

Who Is Best?

Written by May Brown
Illustrated by Jan van der Voo

14

PET DETECTIVE

Use these clues and the big picture to help you.

Clues

1. I am up on a roof.
2. I am behind a fence.
3. I am running away.
4. I am behind a tree.
5. I am puffing smoke.
6. I have a fluffy white tail.
7. I am lying around.
8. I am in the van.
9. I am up a tree.

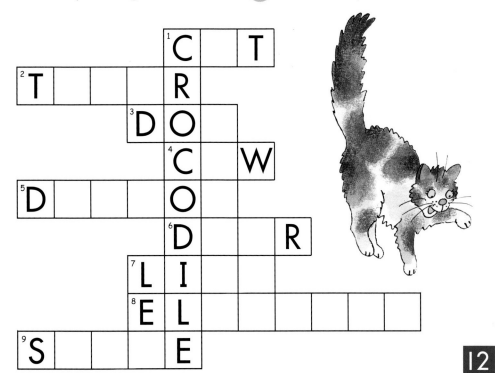

Don't drop your doughnut
in the dishwasher.
Don't drop your doughnut
down the drain.

Don't drop your doughnut
in the dog's dinner.
Don't you dare
drop that doughnut again!

The animals like to dance and sing.
The animals like to do tricks.

"Who is best?" they say.
"Let's see who is the best."

16

The bears dance.

The elephants dance.

The butterflies dance, too.

The owls sing.

18

The monkeys are funny.
Look at Mrs. Giraffe!
The animals all laugh.

21

"Who is best?
Who will win?"
shout the animals.

22

"The bears are best!" says Mrs. Giraffe.

23

Diggy Dog

Written by Martin Bailey ★ Illustrated by Kelvin Hawley

Diggy Dog liked to dig.
He dug holes in chairs.
He dug holes in the floor.

He dug holes in gardens.

He dug holes under fences.

He dug and he dug and he dug.

He dug all the way to the zoo.

"We are not happy,"
said the people.
"That Diggy Dog is no good.
He digs up things."

So the police
took Diggy Dog away.

Pete saw Diggy Dog in the paper.
Pete rang the police.
"Diggy Dog can help me," he said.

Now Diggy Dog helps Pete dig.
He digs and digs and digs.

Tig the Pig

Tig the Pig
likes to dig.

Tig the Pig
finds a wig.

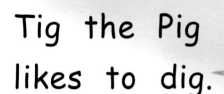

Tig the Pig
likes to jig.

Tig the Pig
is **big, big,**
big!

35

Letters I Know

 Dd Nn

Sounds I Know

 -ig

Words I Know

and	dig	like	say
are	do	me	they
best	dug	my	too
big	he	not	who